MOON IN BEAR'S EYES

*To my brother, Captain Robert, who has the sea in
his eyes, and to his family, Miki, Elina, and Haruna*
SRS

Thanks to Kerry Gunther, Bear Management Specialist for Yellowstone
National Park, for reviewing the manuscript.

Library of Congress Cataloging-in-Publication Data
Swinburne, Stephen R.
Moon in bear's eyes / by Stephen R. Swinburne : illustrated by Crista Forest.
p.   cm.
Summary: Describes a day in the life of a grizzly bear family in Yellowstone's
high country.
ISBN 0-7613-0059-7 (lib. bdg.)
1. Grizzly bear—Yellowstone National Park—Juvenile literature.
[1. Grizzly bear. 2. Bears.] I. Forest, Crista, ill. II. Title.
QL737.C27S95   1998
599.784'09787'52—dc21   97-16038   CIP   AC

Published by The Millbrook Press, Inc.
2 Old New Milford Road, Brookfield, CT 06804

MOON IN BEAR'S EYES

By Stephen R. Swinburne

Illustrated by Crista Forest

THE MILLBROOK PRESS
BROOKFIELD, CONNECTICUT

In the stillness of a wild and
barren mountain ridge, the snow
lies deep. A full moon casts thin,
sharp shadows of spruce trees,
black on white like a zebra's hide.
At the base of one of the old, fallen
spruce trees, a great mound of
snow begins to shudder.

Like sudden thunder, a grizzly
bear explodes in a shower of snow
from the entrance of its den among
the roots of the ancient tree. The
grizzly wags its shaggy pelt and sits
on its haunches, drowsy still.
Silence again. And, then, the
mother grizzly grunts, deep and
soft, "Whoooof."

Two grizzly cubs lope to the entrance of the den and scamper into mother's lap. They look up and see the moon in her eyes.

It is late April in Yellowstone National Park. The bear cubs were born in January, blind and almost naked, the size of kittens. They nursed on the mother's fat-rich milk while she hibernated. The young mother bear has not eaten since October. Six long months.

She sits for a while, adjusting to the light and sounds of the high country. She stares across the valley while the cubs play on her lap and then nurse. The sky reddens into dawn. Nearby, a great gray owl blinks twice and sleeps.

The mother grizzly, who is also called a sow, has lost a lot of weight during her hibernation. She needs to keep up her supply of energy-rich milk so the cubs will survive. She must regain her weight; she must eat. She reads the wind and rises.

Mother grizzly saunters along the crest of the wide ridge. The two bear cubs tumble alongside their mother's legs. A red squirrel tucked in the crotch of a tree freezes while the grizzly family passes beneath. The ridge runs steadily downhill to where spring sunshine melts the deep Yellowstone snow. The mother grizzly rests beside an aspen tree, its trunk the size of a telephone pole. She then rises on hind legs to her full six feet, and reaches high as if to stretch, working her claws by raking them cleanly through the aspen bark; again and again, until the tree bark is shredded and gouged.

The mother grizzly sniffs the wind, and smells the red squirrel hiding in the canopy overhead. She lets it go, for she is not a climber. Her ears hear the new sounds of spring, like the tremble of an aspen leaf brushing in the wind. She listens and watches. A deep rumble comes from her empty belly. Her cubs look up.

She lumbers gradually downward to the meadows and valleys, the cubs trailing at her feet. The family of bears emerges from a spruce and pine wood, entering a bright, greening meadow. A few feet into the field the mother grizzly stops abruptly, so suddenly that the cubs bump headlong into her legs. The grizzly bear shoves her muzzle across the ground and begins swinging her head from side to side, sniffing the earth, tasting the air.

She sweeps forward and with one front paw, shovels up a mound of sod and plants the size of a boulder. She tears apart the soil, the hump of muscles stacked on her back powering her front legs and claws. Mother grizzly begins to pick out juicy, nutritious roots and bulbs of spring beauty. She gorges on the leaves, the buds, the stems, and the roots. Her muzzle and chest become drenched with plant juice and her black, wet nose, smeared with dirt. The bed of wildflowers is soon a plot of stone, rubble, and mud, as if a farmer had tilled there. The bear cubs vault over the muck and mess.

When she can eat no more, she flops in the afternoon sun and shuts her eyes. For the moment, she feels full. The cubs bury their heads in their mother's thick underbelly to nurse. Mother grizzly dozes half awake, one part of her on the edge of deep sleep, the other alert to the rhythmic snuffling noises of her young.

Her eyes open. From somewhere, the faint scent of warm fur wafts into mother grizzly's senses. Her muzzle leads her a few strides to the edge of the field. At a tangle of exposed roots at the base of a large tree she begins to dig. With claws extended, she attacks the moist soil. The cubs watch her closely. In no time, she stops, thrusts her snout into the hole, and pulls out a hibernating ground squirrel. *Crunch, gulp.* The cubs plunge their heads in, too, perhaps to see if they can do the same thing, but come up with faces covered in mud pie.

The long afternoon shadows of lodgepole pine crawl across Yellowstone's high country. A red-tailed hawk catches a current of warm air and, with wing feathers fanned like outspread fingers, rises in widening circles. The hawk screams. The three bears peer skyward to search with their eyes for the maker of the noise.

"Woooof!" Mother grizzly announces that the pace will liven— the bears' easy shuffle turns into long, loping strides. The grizzly family trots over and down the meadow, shuffling around a brush patch, threading past windfalls of pines, making for the river valley far below.

Two miles from the river, long before she can see it or hear the crash of water charging through its rocky channel, mother grizzly smells an elk carcass. She stands on hind legs and stabs the meaty wind with her nose, now blowing square in her face. She drools and then snorts and starts forward, leading the cubs at a brisk pace. Her nose is drawn by the strong scent of winter-killed elk.

The grizzly family halts in the woods at the edge of a clearing. Mother grizzly stands up and parts the leaves to scan the field. She spots the dead elk. It lies alongside the bank of a river booming with snowmelt. Mother grizzly steps into the clearing and rolls slowly forward. The cubs spring after her. She bats them and growls, slapping them back into the bushes.

She steals up to the carcass and rakes the hind flank with her claws, ripping away great chunks of meat. She packs her mouth with elk flesh. The air is thick with elk odor and heavy as stone. With a straight view to the line of trees across the clearing, mother bear senses it is safe for the cubs to join her. She grunts. The cubs bound to her and fall silent as they watch her feast.

Over the thunder of rushing water, the family comes to full alert.

From the shadows of lodgepole pine, fifty feet away, a young male, or boar, grizzly charges the mother and her cubs. The boar grizzly wants the elk for himself, and will eat one or two bear cubs, too, if he can get them. Mother grizzly and the cubs peel away in a mad dash, bounding along the brim of the swollen river. The male grizzly cuts them off. He looms his full height of eight feet, roars, and swipes the air with deadly claws.

The cubs whine, cowering in mother bear's shadow. Mother grizzly's eyes burn. She growls furiously and lunges at the boar with all her power. The impact knocks him down. She stands over him and sinks her teeth into his snout, slashing claws across his muzzle. The boar grizzly bashes his paws against mother grizzly's neck, but she doesn't let go. They roll together, fighting with snapping jaws. The mother's rage is too strong, and the boar weakens. He frees himself, and bellowing in pain and anger, bolts across the meadow to the safety of the woods.

Mother bear nuzzles her young. The cubs soon forget the danger of the encounter and tug on mother bear's long fur with their teeth, pretending to fight. She leads them away from the elk carcass and the boar grizzly, for he may return. There may be other food downriver. She inhales the wind, and the wind tells her to move.

Author's Note

Bears are the largest four-footed carnivores, or meat eaters, on Earth. Three species of bears are found in North America—the brown, the black, and the polar bear. Grizzly bears are a type of brown bear. Grizzlies average eight feet (244 cm) in length and weigh about 790 pounds (350 kilograms). The grizzly bear can outweigh the smaller black bear by more than 200 pounds (90 kilograms). The largest living land carnivore is the Alaskan brown bear, or Kodiak, which reaches a height of ten feet (300 centimeters) and weighs 1,720 pounds (775 kilograms).

Grizzly bears get their name from the white-tipped hairs on their shaggy fur, giving them a frosted or "grizzly" look. They can range in color from cream to cinnamon, from dark brown to black.

Three characteristics identify a grizzly bear in the field. All grizzlies have a large, distinct hump above their shoulders. This shoulder hump is made up of muscles that power the strong front legs and feet for digging. Another feature of the grizzly is its "dish-face" appearance. The grizzly has a high forehead, so seen from the side, the bear's profile is concave, or curved inward. The face of the black bear, on the other hand, is straight. The third characteristic of the grizzly is the long claws on its front feet.

Smell is the grizzly's most important sense. Grizzlies can detect a carcass almost ten miles (16 kilometers) away. An Indian proverb says, "A pine needle falls in the forest. The eagle sees it fall. The deer hears it. The bear smells it." Grizzlies depend on their hearing, too. Their ears, which are three times the size of a human's ear, can often hear danger before it arrives. When hiking through a grizzly bear habitat, be sure to make some noise to alert bears of your whereabouts. Hike in groups of three or more people. A group this size is rarely bothered by bears. Bears see better close up than far away. They can pick up movement very well, and, in most cases, will run away. Bears don't like surprises. They can become unpredictable and dangerous if they are near food or protecting their young.

The first impression of a grizzly bear in the wild is of a slow moving and bulky animal. In fact, grizzlies can run about 35 to 40 miles (55 to 65 kilometers) per hour, as fast as a horse.

Grizzly bears are omnivorous, eating both meat and vegetation. The diet of a grizzly bear includes leaves, roots, berries, insect grubs, small rodents, salmon, and carrion, or dead animal flesh. Grizzlies also eat hoofed mammals such as elk, moose, deer, and bison, taking mostly the sick, injured, and young.

Around September, grizzlies dig their dens and usually go to sleep for the winter in November. Female grizzlies enter the den first and emerge from the den last, while males enter the den later but emerge first.

From January to March, females give birth to from one to four cubs, with two cubs being the average. The young are born with closed eyes, little body hair, and are about ten inches long. Grizzlies wake up and leave their dens in March or April. They mate in May or June. Although grizzly bears mate in the summer, the development of the baby is delayed until late fall. This is perfect timing because the mother begins hibernation in the fall with extra layers of body fat. After mating, the males abandon the females and become dangerous to the cubs once they have been born. Young bears stay with their mothers for two to four years. Grizzlies usually live twenty to thirty years in the wild.

Grizzly bears once lived in most states west of the Mississippi River. Starting in the mid-1800s, western ranchers killed grizzly bears that posed a threat to their sheep and cattle. Today, the grizzly bear's range has shrunk due to the loss of their habitat, and they are now considered a threatened species. About 1,000 grizzly bears remain in the states of Wyoming, Montana, Idaho, and Washington. The wilderness sections of Yellowstone National Park and Glacier National Park are some of the best wild habitats remaining outside Alaska and Canada for the grizzly bear. While grizzlies are scarce in the lower forty-eight states, some 50,000 grizzly bears inhabit western Canada and Alaska.

Learn More About Bears

BOOKS

Fair, Jeff. *Bears For Kids*. Minocqua, WI: NorthWord Press, 1991.

Helmer, Diana Star. *Brown Bears*. New York: Rosen, 1997.

McIntyre, Rick. *Grizzly Cub: Five Years In the Life of a Bear*. Anchorage, AK: Northwest Books, 1990.

Milotte, Elma and Alfred. Toklat: The Story of an Alaskan Grizzly Bear. Anchorage, AK: Northwest Books, 1987.

Patent, Dorothy Hinshaw. *The Way of the Grizzly*. New York: Clarion, 1991.

Pfeffer, Pierre. *Bears: Big and Little*. Ossining, NY: Young Discovery Library, 1989.

Pringle, Laurence. *Bearman: Exploring the World of Black Bears*. New York: Charles Scribner and Sons, 1989.

WEB SITES

The Cub Den Page   www.nature-net.com/bears/cubden.html

Bearwatch   www.bearwatch.org